My Monster

By Declan Harrigan & Jake Biggin

JELLY BEAN BOOKS 2021

A Word from the Author

Dear Reader,

I am honoured to tell the backstory of this little book. *My Monster* was born in the middle of the night in 2018. As I lay awake, I wondered how to support my younger clients, who quite often were anxious about coming in to see me. Counselling can be a very daunting thing and difficult to understand. Most people rely on images from movies, TV and media as a guide, but if truth be told, it's not like this at all.

I offer special thanks to all my younger clients (aged 9 upwards). It's their feedback that helped me shape the concept of the book.

The 'monster' idea actually originated from so many of my clients (aged 5-85) who have often described the 'thing' they are at therapy to work on. Everyone's monster is unique to them, and we all have one.

The aim of this book is to show that no matter what your monster is: be it anxiety, bullying, abuse, bereavement, etc., and no matter what age you are, we all have the ability to take the power back through therapeutic support. Of course, no monster completely disappears. It just stays with us and we learn from it.

Fast forward to 2020. I hadn't read through *My Monster* since 2018 and I wasn't sure of the impact it could make.

Then the world enters a global pandemic and access to face-to-face counselling is temporarily removed. No one was sure how this would affect young people's mental health. It is probably too early to say, but as we come out of lockdown, this book is designed to assist everyone to become more aware of their own monsters. We know they exist, but they don't have to be in control.

Through openness, support and care for ourselves, we can hold our monsters in our hands, rather than them overshadowing us.

Declan Harrigan

My monster wasn't always here.

I laughed and joked, and had no fear.

I played all day, till the sun went down.

No worries, no stresses, and rarely a frown.

But then something happened, and my brain just froze.

Something scary and secret, that nobody knows.

I tried to forget it; I played all day long.

But it wasn't the same. I knew something was wrong.

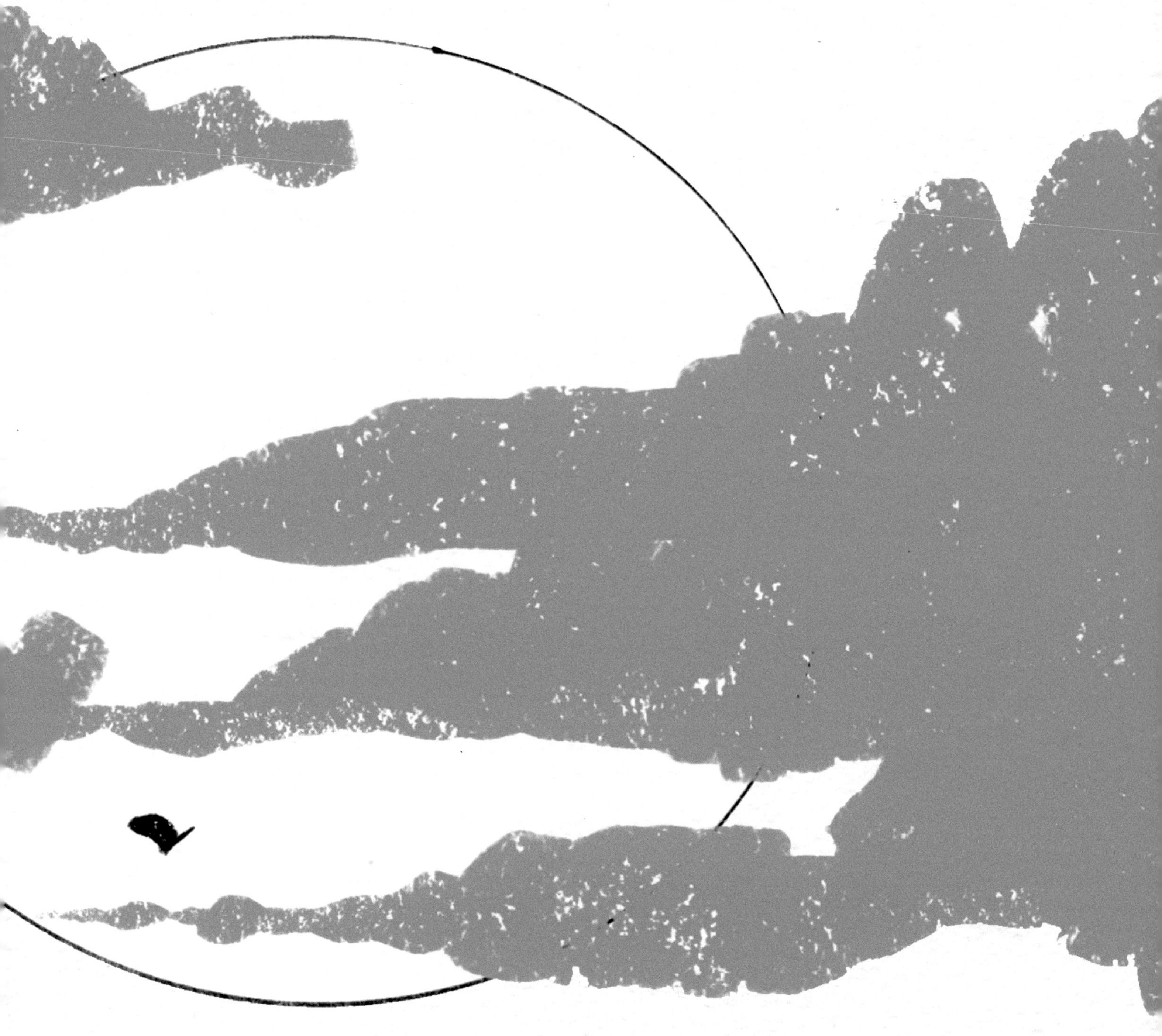

My worry kept building, day after day,

Till it grew to a monster that wouldn't go away.

Its shadow got larger. That's all I could see.

The sun disappeared, and I couldn't run free.

My monster wouldn't let me eat.

My monster wouldn't let me sleep.

I was too afraid to tell someone.

If they laughed at me, it wasn't fun!

'What if they didn't believe me?'

'What if they didn't hear me?'

This made me worry all the time,

Until someone safe saw the sign.

They said that it might help me to talk.

Or maybe we could just go for a walk.

'Counselling,' they said. I replied, 'I'm not mad!

I'm just feeling a little bit sad.'

So I went to counselling, I was nervous and wary.

I thought to myself, *this feels really scary.*

But it wasn't at all, and they helped me relax.

We drew pictures, threw balls, and played with tumbling stacks.

We invited my monster to play as well.

And shared all the thoughts, we felt comfortable to tell.

My monster was sad, as our feelings went deeper.

Sharing my worries made him weaker and weaker.

After a while, my monster got tired.

And my counsellor said, 'He soon will be fired.'

My monster was hungry; he ate sadness for fun.

But I had no more food, and my monster was done.

Now my monster lets me eat.

Now my monster lets me sleep.

The sun's come out. I'm having more fun,

Since I've told my monster to run.

Now my monster's smaller and smaller.

But I'm growing taller and taller.

Soon my monster would disappear.

And like before I'd have no fear.

"An inspiring short story that allows everyone, irrespective of age, to connect with their inner monster and see hope for the future. A wonderful way to introduce the therapeutic journey to recovery. A tool I will most certainly use!"
Louise Scott (Prof Dip Psy C), Psychotherapist
& Director at Mind & Mission

"My Monster *is a valuable introduction to children of the concept of mental health, and that times can be tough. The story affirms to children that this is okay, and helps break down transgenerational, developmental and cultural stigmas.*
Andy Gray, Company Director - ACT Counselling
Services Ltd/Psychotherapist

"This wonderful book is a great way to start a conversation with young people about becoming aware of their minds, and the importance of their mental wellbeing."
Dr Lucy Petro, Cognitive neuroscientist and Cognitive Behavioural Therapist

"I absolutely love this. What struck me was how universal this can be as it doesn't mention one particular challenge. I love the illustrations too as it brings a real sense of anticipation and wondering what's going to happen next."
Dr Fraser Smith, Counselling Psychologist & Founder of Psychology Scotland

"I think this book really breaks down the stigma that can be associated with counselling in a really simple, child friendly way. I would absolutely use it with the children and families that I work with daily."
Natalie Baird, Children & Families Social Worker

"A picture book to help very young children to manage their monsters. Beautifully simple black and white illustrations provide rich metaphor and become more colourful as the monster retreats."
Jeanine Connor, Editor BACP CYPF

Declan Harrigan is a counsellor / psychotherapist, clinical supervisor and trainer. Born in Ireland, he moved to Scotland in 2011, where he set up a children's and young person's charity to provide free counselling to 10-26 year olds. He specialises in work with self-harm, suicidal thoughts / ideation, trauma and anxiety.

Jake Biggin is an artist and illustrator. He studied fine art at Central St Martins in London. A father of two, Jake works in a little box at the end of the garden.

For Sam & Alice

Acknowledgements

To my wife and son who are my inspiration for everything that I do. You are my driving force behind me, and there are no words of thanks or love that can express exactly how much I appreciate all that you do.

To my parents for encouraging me to always follow my dream and to never give up. They taught me that if you strive for the best you will always succeed.

To all the counsellors and psychotherapists who work tirelessly at ensuring that your clients have a safe, non-judgemental and open space to come to on a regular basis (especially through the COVID-19 pandemic). Thank you.

To all the team at S.M.I.L.E Counselling, from the board of trustees, the management, staff, volunteers and trainees. Thank you all for your hard work, dedication and commitment to providing children and young people with the best level of counselling and psychotherapy they deserve.

To the children and young people who specifically inspired me to write this book as a way of demystifying therapy, and for giving me their honest opinion about what might help most for other children and young people. Thank you so much.

And to everyone along the way who have supported me to share the story of 'My Monster'. To the proof readers, and those who challenged certain aspects, which allowed it to evolve to the book it is today. Thank you all for taking the time and patience to read with an open mind.